So, you write poetry?

Are you a poet?

WINDOW SPIT

BY

ALAN DAVID PRITCHARD

Other works:

Poetry
Advancing Backwards – DementedPoet Press

Novel
The Pebble Champion – Kindle Direct

Plays
Red-Handed – LazyBeeScripts

Window Spit
First Published 2017
DementedPoet Press

Cover Photo:

Photographer, D. Sharon Pruitt Owner of Pink Sherbet Photography
Official Website, www.pinksherbet.com

For Dan –

because you probably won't read this

and

for Clem, Fran, Jane, and Preeti –

because you probably will.

Table of Contents

Looking Out

WINDOW SPIT

I saw your Facebook post.
My God, it off-ended me!
There'll be no 'likes' from this finger,
and I'll report your ass, you'll see.

I'll take two hours from my day,
to vent my displeasure supreme,
and let everyone I know know
just how offended I've been.

How dare you have views that are
so very different from mine?
OMG, the way you share and
update them all the time!

It's like you have nothing better to do
than to spend each minute each day
offending decent folk like me
with everything you say!

I have every right to be so terribly put out,
every right to be so very bitter.
The world will soon know how I feel
when I tweet about it on Twitter!

CONCENTRATION BAN

Stop sharing your poetry with us.
We don't want your words.

We want scandal, celebs, memes
and cute pictures of kids or birds

or anything else that is easy to skim
within a second or two.

Don't make us waste precious time
reading stanza after stanza of you

going on and on about this or that.

We only have time for - oh, look -
a cat!

REDUCED TO THIS

They go to an art gallery
to stare at their phones
and then on to a nightclub
where they spend most of the night
dancing with people
who are not there.

They go out on a romantic date –
he plays games,
she takes pictures
of the food they eat
without tasting.

He pays a fortune
to enjoy a holiday alone
and updates messages back
to people who rarely listen.

She sits at a party
texting a person
two seats away.

I cannot touch you
unless you're behind

a screen.

DISTANCE

They come to the park
to sit all alone,
and ignore the swings
to play on their phone.

The merry-go-round
is just a round seat;
only fingers move
over unscuffed feet.

The jungle gym stands –
unwanted statue –
a shell of the past,
with nothing to do.

The ghosts of torn jeans
and laughter-fed falls
echo louder now
than football-led calls.

No bruises, no scrapes,
no calls to come in;
no dares, no races
to see who will win.

So what can they keep
when their days are gone –

what memories of
the way the sun shone?

EX-SMOKER

It takes one minute twenty-four,
exactly,
from your floor
to the building front door
but yet you light your cigarette
in the elevator.

Do you have to?
Really?

My meal costs half a week's wages
and comes in five stages
with ingredients from some distant shore.
The bass, clam-sauce soaked,
will now arrive smoked
because you can't wait
just – what? –
twenty minutes more?

Do you have to?
Really?

The nightclub's abuzz,
you can't move on the floor;
everyone's eager to please.
They've put on Chanel, I've put on Dior;
you've added …
Nicotine Breeze.

Do you have to?
Really?

There's no ashtray in sight
– now there's a clue –
there are even signs
on the door –
big red ones with bold "NO" lines
that you
simply choose to ignore.

Do you have to?
Really?

You accuse me of being selfish,
as I walk away,
and say that I don't understand.
You add that I'm just a cliché
as you light the ciggie in your hand.

This date's a mess,
it's time to go;
please know that this is true:

it's not me, it IS you –

and I have to.
Really.

CONSPIRACY

The way you fell,
like millions before,
was beautifully precise
like shock and awe.

A cascade of catastrophe:
from the top floor
a chaotic concertina
of steel, thermite (and more).

More than ten years have gone,
and the lies still endure
pulverizing the dead,
silencing those who are sure

that your beautiful falling
was no accident, obscure,
but an orchestrated
implosion by those wanting war.

JUST SAYIN'

There were no suicide bombers
before the Twins fell
in those oil-rich lands
that you claimed were hell.

The tyrants there
had ways unique
to keep the peace
that you now seek.

And though many died
on that fateful day
the collateral cost
is the price we all pay.

And don't you dare
with your weapons supreme
claim to be the victim
of some zealots' scheme.

Everything you've done
has just made it worse,
costing more lives, more
freedoms, our purse.

So don't you dare
fight in my freedom's name,
when you're the ones
who created this shame.

SELECTIVE BLEEDING

Two died in a one-armed shop:
hundreds were glued to their screens.

Three runners dead. It was such a shock,
thousands could hear their screams.

Four places were attacked at nine o'clock;
for millions it was too much to bear.

(We covered our photos with tricolored flags to show how
much we care.)

Over a million have died
since this war began,
and thousands are silenced each noon;

hundreds of children
- all by our own hand -
but we won't report on that soon.

Let it happen there,
we just don't care for to make a fuss.

But oh my god
the wars we declare

when it's one of us.

HOT OFF THE PRESS

A celeb was seen in a too-high skirt –
it made the front page of the news.
Another was found too-high in the dirt –
and dead, some said, paying his dues.

A minister sent rude texts to a girl –
the headlines exploded with glee.
Sordid details that'll make your toes curl –
it involves his neighbour, you see.

Also, pictures of giraffes giving birth –
these things are what matter today;
with ten easy steps to decrease your girth –
and five to make your lover stay.

There are football results to shout about –
We'll Twitter and update you soon.
OMG! This morning two yolks came out
when I cracked an egg with a spoon.

Across the ocean in Afghanistan
two children were shot in the face.
It's a war waged by democratic lands
using technology and space.

Collateral damage, an unwritten report:
innocent lives unworthy of even ink, gone;
smothered by noisy indifference

– news and sport –

silenced savagely by those droning on and on.

WHAT JOB THE POET?

How can I possibly know what you're going through?
I've never felt the utter terror common for you,

never felt the sheer hopelessness that can accrue
when the world's indifference cuts sharply into view:

the angry hurl of mortar, the cruel collapse of clay,
the screams, the sirens, the anguish of dismay;

brick-bruised, suffocating dust,
the flames that burn beneath a broken crust;

splattered blood drying on stone –
no, I can never claim to have known

this reality.

Neither have I felt the sun-scorched hell
of sun-dried veins torn from the skull,

and sand-papered tongue in bloated cheek
too dry to cry, too parched to speak –

no, these sensations are foreign to me.

Nor can I know what a dying man will see
as he is hurled face-first into mortality,

as he drops and swirls in the frozen abyss –
no, not yet, not yet, do I know of this.

So what job, then, the poet, and the painter too,
the writer, sculptor and musician who

find it impossible to sit idly by
when the wells of empathy have run dry?

CRISIS

You knocked on my door one day
to ask if you could stay.
I have only one spare room I said,
and you said that's okay.

And in you came, I felt so glad
to have helped a mate.
I changed the sheet,
and cooked some meat,
and offered you a plate.

And then, another knock,
this time, your wife,
and your children, two.
I hope you don't mind, you said,
but what are we to do?

We need a bed, and to be fed,
and somewhere warm to dream.
We've lost our home, we've lost our town,
been bombed to smithereens.

Of course, I said. (I checked my pot,
unsure how to make it more.)
Come in, I said, it's all I've got,
and then more knocks upon the door.

In came her father and her mother
and their cousins too,
plus a dog, a camel, a cat –

and then I saw the queue.

Sorry you said, but what are we to do?

Oh, one more thing, the meal you bring
it's just not made the way we pray,
if you don't mind, if you'd be so kind,
please throw the lot away.

And that cross hung in that den,
it offends our view.
We'll also need the other room,
the one reserved for you.

I know it's harsh, I know it's tough,
but it's not how it seems.
We've lost our home, we've lost our town,
been bombed to smithereens.

THE OTHER SIDE

We cannot go home anymore,
there is no playground safe from hate;
no underground bunker in which we're secure,
nor sanctuary from this bomb-battering state.

Our daughters are wrenched from our hearts,
their horrors too dark to contemplate;
all running away just begins false starts,
all staying, slaying at a relentless rate.

We give what we can to get a boat,
and raft our hopes upon the sea,
relying on profiteers to keep us afloat,
hoping our prophet sees our misery.

And if we get to the other side,
to sidestep our dead upon your shore,
can we expect arms open wide,
from you who felt such horrors before?

Or will you slam the door in our face,
and spit and gossip and sneer
about our clothes, our needs, our race,
the extremes that brought us here?

What if I were your long-lost son,
the daughter you had not seen in years?
Would you be so quick to get a gun,
or herd us away with loaded jeers?

BLOND BOMBSHELL

Your colour-filled trumpets remind me
of black and white rhetoric;
your promises of walls, the threats
of smoke-sodden fences;
your conclusions, the destination:
hate-filled trains of thought, stopping once –
your dramatic pauses unloading
a heavier burden;
departing empty,
full of fear-filled promises.

The overpowering volume
of a marching band going nowhere
inside a tiny church hall:
the trumpeting refrain of one echoing
the prejudice of forefathers;
the barnyard, backstreet
homespun hand-me-down,
small-town, banjo-picking
nit-picking –
cheered on
by those who think
they are the world,
those who think
they have little to lose
like those who chose
to goose step towards
their better tomorrow.

They rejoice in the freedom of choice,
as you lock them in from the outside;
and we – those who shout silently in code –
we despair,
waiting
waiting for the world
to explode.

RECKONING

'Make a difference' –

this insistent plea
is an acronym for insanity;
billionaires and tyrants
make a difference each day –

but beware the spit of a poet with
something to say.

Not so long back then
the pen needed paper
before the words could fly,

but now we can spit
and gob in your eye
and click and send
before a second rolls by

and our phlegm-flavoured
disapproval will cling to the screen,
and harden like your bad habits

if you know what I mean.

And harden and fester
and then petrify –

beware the poet who spits in your eye.

Now our truths can be manufactured
with a tweet and a grin;
immortalized through shares and likes:
voices of reason,
antidotes to spin.

And come the revolution,
you'll be the first to die,

brought down by the mad poets
who spit in your eye.

DARK MATTER

How to see the light
when the darkness is so bright?

The killer whale plays with its prey;
with bleeding eyes, the seal spies
the glare of endless sky
before plunging into familiar inevitability.

The killer laughs at the praying priest;
proclaims god's greatness
as his victim bleeds, sees infinite grace
in the dark space behind his eyes.

The controller of the drone cracks a killer joke about ants;
high-fives his mates as the blinding flash
incinerates children liberated from the shade of the target's
lair.

Half a world away, a teacher shakes his head and smiles,
red-circling all the spelling mistakes
in a student's poem about the importance of faith.

SUPERMARKET CCTV

A little boy – let's not rush past that, please –
possibly four or five,
walks behind his father,
holding both hands.

One leads, focused on
the items his wife ordered him not to forget,
playfully pulling
the most important thing in all their lives;
the other tugs with ...
with all the insistence of one
innocently
testing boundaries, or strength,
or maybe he is just
wishfully pestering
for a more fruitful return to the sweetie aisle.

And then – and this is where
less than a second matters more than eternity –
the boy jerks just a fraction too hard,
too much,
and his father is caught off balance
(maybe the floor cleaner had been too zealous, too eager to
please his boss, or the authorities or the customers, or had
taken too much pride in a job well done) -
and the man slips
...

(there is nobody to blame for this)

and he falls backwards
upon his child,
who breaks his fall,
breaking his neck in the process:
some lifeless thing
that the father scoops up
and comforts in vain.

I cannot imagine his thoughts
before everything is severed.

All that remains is a limp,
eternally-empty
non-responsive thing:
his weight, heavier than guilt,
infinitely unhelpful
and forever tragic;
a tiny, beautiful
former reason to live.

I almost wish someone had come in with a gun,
a knife,
a reason to blame,
to hate,
to make any of this make sense.

But
there is just this:
a shop assistant with a story to tell;
a man whose tomorrow is broken like bone,
a wife who cannot bear to go on –

and an infinitely uncaring camera
which captured it all.

PREDATOR

"We find his banter quite amusing –
why else would we invite
someone like him to our party?"

"He's an uncomplicated lay,
which means I can leave
as soon as it's over – and I do."

"That's not how it is. I blow him
for a tenner and he gives it to me
because I need the money – not because…"

"He's nice. He takes me
for drives to the beach. I think
he would like to be more than just friends."

AFTERMATH

He was twenty-six when he died;
many people cried.
One couldn't make it to the funeral.

They searched for reasons why.
He had met a guy
online, the attraction was mutual.

Sometime later, a mile away,
another hanged himself, 32, gay.
The same site, the same guy, same ritual.

Two is unfair; three, obscene –
an older body floating downstream.
Kind and gentle, an intellectual.

The one who connects sheds no tears.
He loves looking older than his years.
Who cares? As long as it's consensual.

STRANGERS

When God said, "Let there be light,"
the world responded in colours blazing bright.

When God said, "Noah, it's really gonna rain,"
Noah replied, "Lord, I'll fetch my hammers, nails and plane."

When God said, "Moses, take my people, lead them through,"
Moses replied, "Right on, Lord – will do!"

When God said, "Jonah, you'll have a whale of a time, you'll see,"
Jonah replied, "It'll take me a while, but I'll get there –
eventually."

When God said, "David, Goliath is so powerful, so insane,"
David replied, "I don't have muscles, but I'll use my brain."

And when God said, "Mary, Joseph – there's a stable waiting for
you,"
they replied, "Right away, Lord. We will be true."

And when God said, "It's time, it's time, my Son,"
Jesus replied, "Father, Thy will be done."

But now:
when our Lord says, "Help animals captured on their knees,"
we say, "Don't go near them. They have fleas."

But now:
when our world says, "Look after earth, it's all we've got,"
we say, "Cut down trees - build a parking lot."

But now:
when our neighbour says, "My problems always give me
nightmares,"
we say, "Whatever. Tell someone who cares."

Imagine if David had said, "Sorry Lord, I'm busy today."
Imagine if Noah said, "I can swim. Go away."
Imagine if Moses was too lazy to walk.
Imagine if Jonah refused to talk.

Imagine, if, when our lives face dangers,
God replies, "Sorry – I don't talk to strangers."

RESPONSIBILITY

We all cry
we all die
we all laugh
we all wonder why

we all lie
we all bleed
we all fall
we all need

we all feed
we all fret
we all love
we all forget

we all share
the tears
of tomorrow's children.

Looking In

THIS OTHER LOVE

(This is not a poem about a cat)

Mostly seen through allergic eyes;
avoided –
late-night cries, despised.
You were just there on a wall.

Those who doted on you, bewitched,
belittled –
I bitched, red-eye itched.
I never liked you at all.

I preferred the other one;
tail-wagger :
Fun! It fetched. We'd run.
You never answered my call.

Now we share a devoted place.
Confronted
by your space, scent, trace,
I am beginning to fall

for all your cuddle-purring charm:
fur-nuzzling,
in my arms, your calm
enchantment, my world, enthralled.

Soft punching with your gentle paw:
feeding time.
For sure, can't ignore;
I now serve this master small.

REFLECTION

Who is that man jeering at me
through spit-splattered window
with his snot-encrusted finger
pointing, pointing?

Who does he think he is?

(He looks vaguely familiar,
like someone I grew
apart with.)

Who is he to stare,
to glare,
to spare no camaraderie,
no sympathy,
no acknowledgement
of familiarity?

(I know those eyes.
He is everything I despise.)

Look at him judging everything
I do because he believes
he now knows better.

(I won't open the door to him.
I have absolutely nothing to say.)

I have tried throwing poetry at him
- but he won't go away.

I NEED TO KNOW

So you aren't a real poet?

No. I just take words and kick them at imaginary goalposts
spray-painted against the rough brickwork of my memory,
like a poor kid with dirty feet and a squalid imagination
penalty kicking at the noise of jumbled graffiti
mindlessly messing about in a
concrete makeshift playground.

So your words aren't poetry?

No, my words are vomit that I smear with newspaper
to make patterns to delight the squeamish,
and as the rains of some other experience
shove them towards the drains,
the implications of change
become something
to momentarily consider.

So this isn't a poem?

No, this is exactly as much of a poem as the dirty
shark-shaped cloud is a real fish that you catch
with a broken umbrella in the shade of a
boring summer's haze. I am glad I
could console you with the
quiet certainty
of my dirty
lies.

So you aren't real?

Yes.

PARTY

I don't get asked out much these days –
which is why even I
am surprised I'm here.

I have probably said no too often before.

I wonder (briefly)
if they think I am rude,
choosing to unwittingly ignore
invitations to move to music,
or chat with some bore
in a cluttered kitchen

(which despite my unsolicited efforts,
will still be a mission to clean
when the guests have gone).

They don't get that I prefer
dancing silently
to a quieter noise.

The monkey holds the magnets,
and, letting go,
delights in the soft
clink
of attraction.

Bemused that a gentle pinch
is enough to separate
the bewildering bond,
his fingers part,

his brow question marks
as the metals embrace without his doing -
like a baby rushing unquestioningly
back into the arms of his mother.

This brings him joy.

Curiosity – what else? –
makes him wonder
what will happen if
the polarity of one is reversed ...
and, after some trial,
his delight turns to satisfaction
when, with a gentle prod,
he can use one
to make the other move
away without touching –
the repulsion of prey sensing
the predator's pounce.

This almost
irresistible inevitability
captivates him:
a fascinating frisson,
a terrible attraction –

like a child whose Lego creation
creates itself when he lets go
of the blueprint in his mind.

"You're very quiet tonight.
What's on your mind?"

"Magnets," I reply,
moving to the balcony
to play with the monkeys
alone in the trees.

OCD

Is it a compulsive need to be heard,

this obsessive word-piling,
this absurd semantic filing,
this eccentric tic to make ideas
stick in just the right way?

Or maybe it's something
that needs to be said,
that ought to be bled
like carcasses of thought
hunter-caught
and carved for display?

Or maybe the words
are just

magnets of gladness
attracted to sadness,
had-ness?
fad-ness?
madness?

Repelled by prose,
only the poet knows

what they are forced to say.

THE CHOSEN FEW

We are the lines that they could not use.
We are
the words that they chose not to choose.

Rejected by reason or banished by beat,
we are
marooned by meter, the stress of feet.

Unable to compete or to be true,
we are
too big for Cinderella's shoe.

We inhabit a world of lost socks and missed trains.
We are
ill-fitting similes and forgotten refrains.

The words you really wanted to say,
we are
the ones that got away.

You were too fussy, or strict, or hopelessly inept.
We are
orphaned refugees that need to be kept

slaves ready for another muse to inspect.
We are
waiting, waiting for a poet to select.

THE LETTING GO

Let go, the poem cried,
and for goodness' sake, stop touching me.

My hair is fine just as it is –
I like it looking scruffy.

You don't have to dress me up so,
it's not the queen we'll see.

I want to run in the playground of thought,
without rhyme or symmetry.

Oh, why do you have to polish my shoes?
Let me go barefoot and free -

I want to be play, naked and crude,
like before you gave birth to me.

SHALLOW

I fuckin' hate poetry –
I really do –
or at least the poetry I consider
to be pretentiously bad:
those soaked in cliché
and self-imposed catharsis ...

You are in a city you hardly know
with people who have no idea who you are.
They sit with their backs to me;
yours is the face I see.

You nod, you listen,
and I turn away when eye
contact is made,
because you are the subject of this piece
and anything more than that
would just be awkwardly unnecessary.

I am enjoying interpreting your reality
without the burden of veracity.

I imagine you would rather be
with those your own age somewhere else
talking about other things
without the need for you to pretend to be
interested, or interesting.

They talk at you, and I guess you're
suppressing the need to yawn,
the urge to leave without apology.
(Your fake smile, again.)

They are probably your older colleagues,
and you probably want to go into the city
to meet girls whose names you
probably won't want to remember.

I wonder if you are suppressing, too,
the urge to rant and toss the table
like a teenager sore-losing
a boring board game.

Or perhaps this is not the case
– the truth is entirely irrelevant –
because we haven't made eye contact,
and I do not wish to know your name ...

so I go back to writing about
the shit poetry of others,
quietly hoping
to catch the eye
of someone cute enough
to ask me what I am doing.

BEST LEFT ALONE

A word

even a hello –
is something I'd flinch from,
like one beaten
by more than words,
who cowers
when someone reaches up
just to shake someone's hand.

Such is the raw need
to be left alone in the crowd.

When genial conversation
feels like a stick
punishing the silence –
and the bare minimum response,
cold-shouldered,
invites intrusive concern,
felt as deliberate provocation.

This towards people who wish me no ill.
And who forgive me and understand anyway.

And who tell me not to worry when I apologize later.

Because worrying is the inevitable consequence –
the inevitable irony.

Do we all sometimes feel this way?
This contempt for those who dare intrude
on our self-imposed public exile?

Or is it just – and this is where I falter –
is it just my own particular grumpy selfishness,
this dunce-like dance into the corner,
into the shadows of a crowded space?

I have come out into the noise of convergence just to be
seen to be
wanting to be left alone.

It would have been way
less complicated
to have stayed at home.

But who, then, would have witnessed
my overwhelming desire
to be ignored?

NOTE TO SELF

I hate you
because you force me
to look at things from your point of view
but
you resist the urge
to see things from mine.

I love being with you,
spending time just being,
but
when you hide away
and shirk from company,
and I need to seek you out
hoping for that smile,
your patient indifference
breaks my heart,
almost.

I have so much to tell you.

IMPOTENT

Right now,
I could be
shopping for that lady
whose flat at the end of the hall
smells of unwanted meals,
unwanted smells that stain the walls
like regret.

Right now,
I could be
reading hopeless stories
about distracting adventures to kids
who won't be here next week,
or tomorrow;
or telling jokes, or performing
the kind of magic that delights
but does not fool anybody.

Right now,
I could be shovelling smelly shit
for the shelter downtown,
while listening to the distracting banter
of volunteers about the hopelessly
inadequate funding for unwanted pets –
and the unnecessary need
to put so many of them down.

Or maybe I could just be walking,
simply smiling for strangers
who may simply have had a rather bad day.

Instead,
right now,
I am staring at the walls,
still waiting
for the phone to ring
because you said you would call.

SEISMIC

A side remark over dinner with friends,
barely perceptible,
the tiniest crack,
begins the fissure that snakes
through our bedtime silence.

It led to a joke at my expense,
a minor commentary,
almost - and I say almost
because I have replayed it so often
in the car on the way home - witty;
a seemingly insignificant lightning bolt
that I felt from a distance.

Oh honey, I was only joking,
will probably be your response if confronted,
because for you a slip of the chisel is just a mishap -
but I know better than to prove me right,
so instead I prepare to stare at the hairline cracks
in the walls as you prepare for sleep.

It is not that I am angry; I'm not –
an obligatory kiss on the cheek before you
embed yourself in your side,
while I feel inside
the tectonic shift that widens
as the night begins to heave us apart:

the aftershock of a throwaway comment;
the rift of an unhealable scar.

You chose to publicly poke
at something which should have been
spoken about privately – a quiet criticism –
thrown like a stone directly at me
which we all found funny,
and even I smiled –
before changing the subject

to the tragedy of a nearby earthquake,
and the unlikelihood of there being many survivors.

SOCIOPATH

I am vaguely amused:
you are offended
because I wilfully choose
to enjoy my own company.
Honestly,
the conversations
I have with myself
are more interesting
than the dialogues
I have with you.

LONELY

You are not allowed to feel
so down;
there's folks with stuff worse than you –
you might be feeling hard done by,
but you'll wake tomorrow, blue.

And the azure sky
that you choose to ignore,
will be denied to
so many who
take their last breath tonight,
or who
will feel the dark of some life almost lost,
not knowing the cost
of tomorrow's light.

Look at you
feeling so very sorry for yourself
when there are so many who
would relish your greeting,
your ear,
your moment's diversion
from the unbearable
fear of whatever it is that stops
them from reaching out
to embrace those who
may have it worse.

So it essentially
comes down to this:

your choosing
to be
so terribly
alone.

SHUT THE FUCK UP

You're not allowed to own these feelings;
think of the women whose children are dead,
and the drones and the bombs that
splatter kittens and grandmothers
and the terror that feeds on dread.

Your bad day – your colleague is a cunt –
means you still go home to a home intact,
and your bruised ego or damaged pride
- or whatever the fuck it is that,
omg, grieves you so – would be
infinitely forgotten
the second your kid is blown to bits
by some zealous fanatic with a slogan
and his mission from god.

So do not own these feelings.
You are not allowed to feel shit.
Take responsibility for the shit choices
you have made –
and fucking deal with it.

RELIC

We are now the other them,
and the them we think they are
exist in some other playground.

Their doors are opened through screens;
ours were opened using
keys of chance, the whims of romance,

rejections before last dance,
the Chinese whispers as we
passed our hearts on papers in class.

We loved so and so because
they smiled at us first, hearts burst,
friends cursed, tears were hot and real.

We dated, held hands for weeks
stole clumsy kisses before
declaring love with breathless cheeks.

We went for walks, had long talks,
whispered over chocolate shake
the promises we could not keep.

They don't glance up from their phones,
flick left, right, choose whom to meet.

We are now the other them,
the ones we'd point at in the street.

PIVOT POINT

Is there more behind than there is ahead?
And either way, which will be the greater?

This is a moment neither of regret,
nor of loaded judgement burdened by need.

The birdsong is sometimes squashed by traffic;
the clouds beyond this summer Sunday's street

are heavy; the break from the showers, welcomed.
Again, I have left my raincoat at home.

This real-life interlude isn't so bad;
this cafe's breeze is better than a screen.

Newlyweds sit opposite, holding hands;
she's pregnant, he discusses a new job.

My regular waiter brings the usual;
he knows I rarely want anything new.

So there's this now, this monumental scene:
the couple, the waiter, the elephant,
me.

FUTILITY

Perpetually
letting
go:
a shell
turning
inside
out
laying
hollowness
bare,
spilling
definition –
yet,
it
remains
an
emptiness
invaded
once more
by the
silence
of
strangers,

screaming.

SHARK

I thought the shadow
was that of my canoe –
the inevitable consequence
of rowing in the sunshine,
of waving at those on the sand,
of looking ahead,
of keeping my chin up.

The fins should have given it away,
but to me it was just the silhouette
of a simile lurking beneath the surface,
something occasionally glimpsed at,
the necessary exhaust of effort.

The stalking should have given it away,
the constant circling,
but I saw it only as the inevitable contrast
of a sunburnt smile.
The yin, the yang,
the need to shit after a hearty feast.

I am not sure when I realised
the dark shape was hungry
for more than the chase,
when I knew
I'd be devoured as soon as
the smile drained from my face,
when I was sure

the race to out-row the shadow
would end with my dropping the oar.

The intense effort
to keep rowing,
to keep waving,
to keep keeping my chin up,
to keep being grateful
I could still move forward
feeling the sun
when others were floundering
(or worse
had sunk to become fuel
for some deeper force)
is
exhausting.

"What's your problem?"
they spit.
"You need to sort
out your shit."

There is blood in the water.

SMUDGE

The lens is smeared:
the murk offers no reflection
other than a lumpy grumpy gripe
about the lunacy of others
seen from behind a screen.

Wiping it clean
only makes things worse,
like putting on the windscreen wipers
during a locust swarm.

And stepping outside
to look back in
allows absolutely no insight,
other than the obvious.

Now the late frost has come to stay.
Your neighbour's roof looks frail.

There is no warmth in rhyme.

PUT DOWN

Put down your words,
mister poet man,
this is not the time to rhyme;
not the time to comment
about the hardship of a neighbour's broken ceiling

(although there is a certain insistent
splendour about the winter sun's
peacock-like splinter through
his fragmented roof)
– stop.

Your attention is needed elsewhere now.

Lay down your similes and schemes.
Your insight won't warm
his shivering child, won't shield him
from the chill,

won't shield you from the fallout
of beautifully phrased sympathy.

Your hands are needed elsewhere now.

If you have enjoyed this work, please leave a positive review on Amazon.

Also, if you would like to view internationally-acclaimed video poems from this collection, please visit:

www.alandavidpritchard.com

or

subscribe to my YouTube page:

www.youtube.com/user/MrAlanDavidPritchard

Thank you!

THE END

www.ingramcontent.com/pod-product-compliance
Lightning Source LLC
Chambersburg PA
CBHW061716130726
47996CB00006B/2342